PREHISTORIC!

DINOSAURS
OF THE CRETACEOUS

by
David West

Smart Apple Media

Published by Smart Apple Media, an imprint of Black Rabbit Books
P.O. Box 3263, Mankato, Minnesota 56002
www.blackrabbitbooks.com

Produced by David West ⚤ Children's Books
6 Princeton Court, 55 Felsham Road, London SW15 1AZ

Designed and illustrated by David West

Special thanks to Dr. Ron Blakey for the maps on page 4 & 5

Library of Congress Cataloging-in-Publication Data

West, David, 1956- author.
 Dinosaurs of the Cretaceous / David West.
    pages cm. -- (Prehistoric!)
 Audience: Grade 4 to 6.
 Includes index.
 ISBN 978-1-62588-085-7 (library binding)
 ISBN 978-1-62588-112-0 (paperback)
 1. Dinosaurs--Juvenile literature. 2. Paleontology--Cretaceous--Juvenile literature. I. Title.
 QE861.5.W493 2015
 560.177--dc23
                                        2013038761

Printed in China
CPSIA compliance information: DWCB14CP
010114

9 8 7 6 5 4 3 2 1

Contents

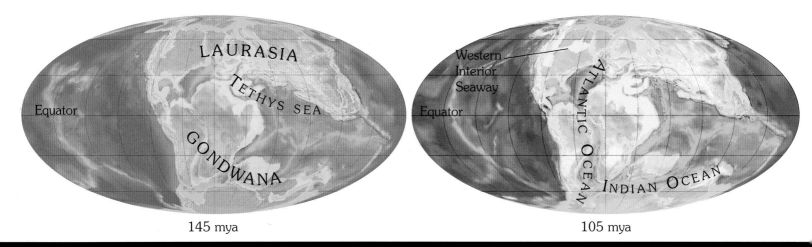

145 mya

105 mya

EARLY CRETACEOUS

Temperatures become cooler resulting in snowfall at high altitudes.

138 mya Temperatures rise and remain high due to intense volcanic activity.

Sea surface temperatures may have been 31 °F (17 °C) warmer than today.

The Cretaceous Period

During this period, the supercontinents of Laurasia and Gondwana continued to break up into present day continents although their positions were very different at the time. The Atlantic and Indian Oceans were newly formed, and the Tethys Sea continued to narrow. As sea levels rose, shallow seas called the Western Interior Seaway appeared across North America and Europe. The period ended with the **Cretaceous– Paleogene (K–Pg) extinction event**.

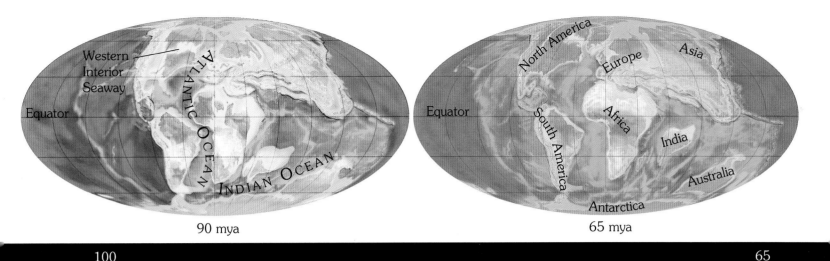

91 mya Lack of oxygen in oceans causes extinction of **ichthyosaurs**.

65 mya The Cretaceous–Paleogene (K–Pg) extinction event killed off as much as 75% of plant and animal species on Earth, including all dinosaurs.

LIFE DURING THE CRETACEOUS PERIOD

On land, mammals were relatively small and still evolving. The dinosaurs remained the dominant species. Huge **carnivores** such as *Tyrannosaurus rex* and *Giganotosaurus* appeared. Giant **sauropods,** called titanosaurs, appeared in the southern continents. Herd-dwelling **ornithischians**, such as *Iguanodon*, spread everywhere. Vast herds of horned dinosaurs such as *Triceratops* lived in the northern continents. The feathered dinosaur group **maniraptora** appeared, which was a transition between dinosaurs and birds. **Pterosaurs** were common. Some grew to enormous sizes but faced growing competition from the evolving bird population. Marine reptiles included ichthyosaurs, **plesiosaurs**, and **mosasaurs**.

An Austroraptor approaches a group of **titanosaurs** called Saltasauruses from South America 80 million years ago.

Concavenator

One of the strangest **fossil** finds in recent years is that of a medium-sized theropod called *Concavenator*. Its name means "Cuenca hunter" after the place in Spain where it was found.

Concavenator had a strange hump on its back above its hips. Scientists are unsure of its purpose. It may have been an area that stored fat for lean times when prey animals were few and far between. Feather quills grew from its forearms. The quills may have been used for display

6

A *Polacanthus* (1) is taken by surprise by a *Concavenator* (2) in this scene from early Cretaceous Europe. *Pelecanimimuses* (3) and *Hypsilophodons* (4) who have been drinking at a spring flee in terror.

during mating rituals. The early spiked, plant-eating Polacanthus also lived in Europe at that time. Its thick, armored plates and spikes were an effective defense against predators. Smaller dinosaurs such as the **ornithomimosaur**, *Pelecanimimus*, and the **ornithopod**, *Hypsilophodon*, were also present.

Concavenator grew to about 19.7 feet (6 m) long and weighed about 2 tons (1.8 mt).

Caudipteryx

Caudipteryx, which means "tail feather," was a small **theropod** dinosaur that was remarkably bird-like in appearance. It lived about 125 million years ago in what is China today.

Caudipteryx's body was covered in soft, downy feathers, and its arms and tail had longer primary feathers. With its beaklike mouth, it was probably an **omnivore** feeding on plants, small lizards, and insects. Another feathered dinosaur living at the same time was *Beipiaosaurus*.

A pair of *Caudipteryxes* (1) run in front of a group of *Altirhinuses* (2) who arrive to feed on cycads. A *Beipiaosaurus* (3) runs alongside a family of *Psittacosauruses* (4). A *Microrapator* (5) glides through the air. *Zhenyuanopteruses* (6) fly to feeding grounds.

This plant eater was a **therizinosaur**. Smaller **herbivores** such as *Psittacosaurus* lived alongside larger ones such as *Altirhinus*. This giant **iguanodont** had a large nasal sack that could expand like elephant seals' noses. Small dinosaurs called *Microraptors* could glide through the air, keeping safe from ground-based predators.

Caudipteryx grew to 40 inches (1 m) long and weighed about 20 pounds (9.1 kg).

3

Suchomimus

Suchomimus, meaning "crocodile mimic," was a giant theropod living in North Africa during the early Cretaceous. It was a member of the **spinosaurid** family of dinosaurs which were specialized hunters.

Suchomimus's skull was long and narrow similar to a crocodile. The jaws had about 130 teeth that were pointed and curved slightly backward. **Paleontologists** think this dinosaur fed on fish and other aquatic animals just like a crocodile. Living alongside *Suchomimus* was

A *Suchomimus* (1) rears away from an attack by a *Sarcosuchus* (2) in a swamp in what is today Niger. A group of *Lurdusauruses* (3) turn to flee from the danger. In the background, a herd of *Ouranosauruses* (4) make their way to the water's edge to drink.

a distant relative of the crocodile, *Sarcosuchus*. This monster grew to 36 feet (11 m) and was capable of killing the giant *Suchomimus*. It probably snacked on the iguanodonts, *Ouranosaurus*, and *Lurdusaurus*. *Lurdusaurus* was over 30 feet (9 m) long and weighed about 2.5 tons (2.3 mt). Scientists think it may have had a lifestyle similar to hippos, spending most of its time in water.

Suchomimus was around 36 feet (11 m) in length and weighed up to 4 tons (3.6 mt).

4

5

3

Deinonychus

Deinonychus means "terrible claw" due to its vicious scythe-like claw on each foot. Its fossils, dating back to the early Cretaceous, have been found in the states of Montana, Wyoming, and Oklahoma.

Although it was not a large dinosaur, *Deinonychus* was a ferocious predator that probably hunted in packs like modern-day wolves. A swift runner, it had a stabbing claw on each foot that it kept raised off the ground when it ran. It would pounce on its prey, grabbing with its

By a river delta close to the sea, a *Tenontosaurus* (1) flees for its life from a pack of *Deinonychuses* (2). A well-armored *Sauropelta* (3) is ignored by the predators. In the background, *Acrocanthosauruses* (4) chase after a pair of *Sauroposeidons* (5).

clawed hands while it stabbed the prey with its foot claws. It might have hunted dinosaurs such as the **nodosaurid**, *Sauropelta,* and the iguanodont, *Tenontosaurus.* The much larger predator, *Acrocanthosaurus* shared the environment. This giant theropod, which grew to about 40 feet (12 m), hunted the sauropod, *Astrodon,* and possibly the much larger *Sauroposeidon.*

Deinonychus grew to about 11.2 feet (3.4 m) long and weighed about 150 pounds (68 kg).

13

Mapusaurus

Mapusaurus was a large **carnosaur** living in South America during the late Cretaceous period. Its name means "earth lizard."

Mapusaurus was similar in size and closely related to *Giganotosaurus*, one of the largest known predators on land. Several individuals have been found together in fossil bone beds. Paleontologists think that this may indicate that *Mapusaurus* hunted in packs. This would have been necessary to take down a large sauropod such as *Argentinosaurus*.

A *Skorpiovenator* (1) was lucky and killed a juvenile from the migrating herd of *Argentinosauruses* (2) but its luck is about to run out. A pair of *Mapusauruses* (3) are about to steal the *Skorpiovenator*'s kill.

This massive titanosaur grew to 98 feet (30 m) in length and weighed 80 tons (73 mt). It is likely that *Mapusaurus* would have singled out old, injured, or juveniles to attack. It also lived off **carrion** and used its large size to steal the kills from smaller predators such as *Skorpiovenator*, which grew to half the size of *Mapusaurus*.

Mapusaurus reached a length of 33 feet (10.2 m) and weighed about 3.3 tons (3 mt).

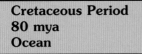

Archelon

Archelon was the largest turtle to have roamed the seas. Its name means "ruler turtle" and it lived in the oceans of the Late Cretaceous.

Archelon probably fed on squid, jellyfish, fish, and **ammonites** by biting through their shells with its powerful beak. Like modern turtles, it would have moved onto land to lay its eggs in sandy hollows that were dug out with its powerful flippers. Scientists think these massive creatures lived for more than 100 years. Due to their size they were

An *Archelon* (1) swims past a pair of *Coelacanthuses* (2) as it feeds on ammonites (3). *Hesperornis* (4) dive for small fish keeping away from the giant *Tylosaurus* (5), which is attacking an *Elasmosaurus* (6) in this ocean image from the late Cretaceous.

attacked only by large sharks and mosasaurs such as *Tylosaurus*. These ferocious marine lizards were the top predators of their day. Their varied diet included fish such as *Coelacanthus*, sharks, smaller mosasaurs, plesiosaurs such as *Elasmosaurus*, and flightless birds such as *Hesperornis*.

Archelon grew up to 13.1 feet (4 m) long and weighed 2.5 tons (2.3 mt).

Parasaurolophus

Parasaurolophus means "near crested lizard." It is a member of the duck-billed family of **hadrosaurs** that had hollow crests. They lived in North America during the late Cretaceous period.

Like all hadrosaurs, *Parasaurolophus* had a beak-shaped mouth like a duck. It used it to trim and strip vegetation from plants before chewing with teeth in the back of its mouth. It also had a long, hollow crest that grew from the back of its skull. Paleontologists think the hollow

18

Parasaurolophuses (1) look up from feeding as a *Corythosaurus* (2) bellows out a warning. It has seen a *Gorgosaurus* (3) about to attack some feeding *Lambeosauruses* (4). A pair of *Styracosauruses* (5) hear the warning and begin to move to safety.

chambers inside the crests were used to make special sounds. Other hadrosaurs with hollow crests lived alongside *Parasaurolophus*. These include *Lambeosaurus* and *Corythosaurus*. Each had its own individual style of crest and probably its own sounds, too. Hadrosaurs were top on the menu for predators such as *Albertosaurus* (see pages 22–23) and *Gorgosaurus*.

Parasaurolophus grew up to 30 feet (9.1 m) long and weighed 4.4 tons (4 mt).

1

Troodon

Troodon was a small theropod living in North America during the late Cretaceous period. Its name means "wounding tooth" due to the serrations on its teeth indicating it was a meat eater. Scientists now think it was probably an omnivore as similar serrations have been found on herbivores' teeth.

Troodon had long, slender legs, which suggest it was a swift runner. It had a sharp, sickle claw on each foot that was raised off the ground

Maiasaura (1) tend their nests and hatchlings on the edge of a nesting colony. In the foreground, a hungry *Troodon* (2) threatens a *Chirostenotes* (3) that has stolen an egg from an abandoned nest. *Einiosauruses* (4) wander by in the background.

when it ran. It had large eyes and could probably see well in the dark and may have hunted at night. *Troodon* lived alongside the **oviraptorid**, *Chirostenotes*. This omnivorous dinosaur was of similar size and might have fed on stolen *Maiasaura* eggs. *Maiasaura* lived in herds and raised their young in nesting colonies. **Ceratopsid** dinosaurs, with hooked horns called *Einiosaurus*, were also present.

Troodon was about 7.9 feet (2.4 m) long and weighed about 110 pounds (49.9 kg).

Edmontosaurus

Edmontosaurus was a large duck-billed dinosaur of the hadrosaur family. Its name means "Edmonton lizard" after the city in Canada, which is close to where its fossils were found.

Edmontosaurus was a herbivore that lived in coastal regions. It used its broad beak to strip off the more nutritious leaves and shoots from plants and then chewed them with its battery of teeth. Based on fossil finds, it may have lived in groups and might have been migratory.

Edmontosauruses (1) flee from a hungry *Albertosaurus* (2). A *Euoplocephalus* (3) is surprised and joins the stampede with a family of *Pachyrhinosauruses* (4). In the distance, a group of *Saurolophuses* (5) look for an escape route.

It could move on two legs or four and could run swiftly from predators such as *Albertosaurus*. This large **tyrannosaur** hunted the many hadrosaurs in the region including *Edmontosaurus* and *Saurolophus*. Rarer dinosaurs such as the ankylosaur, *Euoplocephalus,* and the ceratopsid, *Pachyrhinosaurus,* may also have been on the menu.

Edmontosaurus grew to 39 feet (12 m) long and weighed about 4.4 tons (4 mt).

Alioramus

Alioramus was a tyrannosaurid dinosaur. Related to *Tarbosaurus*, it lived in Asia during the late Cretaceous period. Its name means "different branch" because it differs from other branches of the tyrannosaur family.

Smaller than *Tarbosaurus*, *Alioramus* is recognized by the five ridges on its nose. Its mouth was crammed with more sharp teeth than any other tyrannosaur. It lived alongside *Tarbosaurus*, which grew to 40 feet (12.2 m) long and weighed up to 6 tons (5.4 mt). It was the top

An *Alioramus* (1) reluctantly backs away from its kill, a *Saurolophus* (2), as a large *Tarbosaurus* (3) moves in to steal it. *Mononykuses* (4) run for their lives as do three *Deinocheiruses* (5) in the background.

predator of its time, living in a flood plain with numerous rivers. The environment was populated with many different types of dinosaurs including sauropods such as *Nemegtosaurus*, therizinosaurs, ornithomimosaurs such as *Deinocheirus*, and a strange, small theropod called *Mononykus*. Its name means "one claw" as it only had one claw on each arm.

Alioramus grew to 20 feet (6.1 m) long and weighed about 1,000 pounds (454 kg).

Velociraptor

Velociraptor, meaning "swift seizer," was a **dromaeosaur** that lived during the late Cretaceous period in what is today Mongolia.

Velociraptor had large hands with three curved claws. Each foot had a large, sickle-shaped claw—typical of dromaeosaurs such as *Deinonychus* (see pages 12–13). This enlarged claw could be over 2.6 inches (6.5 cm) long and was used to kill its prey by using a stabbing motion. A fast runner, its long tail kept it balanced. It is likely to have

26

As a sandstorm approaches, a pack of *Velociraptors* (1) look for a likely victim as they skirt a *Protoceratops* (2) nesting site. A fossil was created when a sandbank buried a *Velociraptor* locked in combat with a *Protoceratops*. It was found in Mongolia in 1971.

been covered in feathers for warmth and display purposes. *Velociraptors* lived and hunted in packs. Like most predators, they were opportunists, stealing eggs from dinosaurs such as *Protoceratops*. These small ceratopsid dinosaurs were likely prey for *Velociraptors*. However, their large neck frills and powerful jaws with sharp beaks provided good defense against predators.

Velociraptor grew to 6.7 feet (2 m) long and weighed up to 33 pounds (15 kg).

Tyrannosaurus

Tyrannosaurus rex, the most famous of all dinosaurs, lived in North America during the late Cretaceous period. Its name means "tyrant lizard king" and it was one of the largest predators of its time.

Tyrannosaurus had a massive skull that was balanced by a long, muscular tail. Its powerful jaws were crammed with 12-inch (30 cm) long teeth that were serrated like a saw. The power of its bite could rip into flesh and crush bone. *Tyrannosaurus* could run at a top speed of

28

A hungry *Tyrannosaurus* (1) is beaten back by a *Triceratops* (2). As the *Dracorexes* (3) flee, an *Ankylosaurus* (4) moves away. In the distance, a *Quetzalcoatlus* (6) watches *Pachycephalosauruses* (5) spar with each other for mating rites.

25 miles per hour (40 km/h)—as fast as a top sprinter. Its prey included carrion and plant-eating dinosaurs such as *Triceratops* and *Ankylosaurus*. Bone-headed **pachycephalosaurs** shared the environment. These included the small *Dracorex* as well as the larger *Pachycephalosaurus*.

Tyrannosaurus grew to 40 feet (12.2 m) long and weighed 7.5 tons (6.8 mt).

Animal Listing

Other animals that appear in the scenes.

Acrocanthosaurus
(pp. 12–13)
carnosaur
40 feet (12.2 m) long
North America

Albertosaurus
(pp. 22–23)
tyrannosaur
30 feet (9.1 m) long
North America

Alioramus
(pp. 24–25)
tyrannosaur
20 feet (6.1 m) long
Asia

Altirhinus
(pp. 8–9)
iguanodont
21 feet (6.4 m) long
Asia

Ankylosaurus
(pp. 28–29)
ankylosaur
30 feet (9.1 m) long
North America

Argentinosaurus
(pp. 14–15)
titanosaur
115 feet (35 m) long
South America

Austroraptor
(pp. 4–5)
dromaeosaur
16 feet (4.9 m) long
South America

Beipiaosaurus
(pp. 8–9)
therizinosaur
7 feet (2.1 m) long
Asia

Chirostenotes
(pp. 20–21)
oviraptorid
6.6 feet (2 m) long
North America

Coelacanthus
(pp. 16–17)
fish
3.3 feet (1 m) long
Oceans

Corythosaurus
(pp. 18–19)
hadrosaur
33 feet (10 m) long
North America

Deinocheirus
(pp. 24–25)
ornithomimosaur
33 feet (10 m) long
Asia

Deinonychus
(pp. 12–13)
dromaeosaur
11 feet (3.4 m) long
North America

Dracorex
(pp. 28–29)
pachycephalosaur
10 feet (3 m) long
North America

Einiosaurus
(pp. 20–21)
ceratopsid
15 feet (4.6 m) long
North America

Elasmosaurus
(pp. 16–17)
plesiosaur
46 feet (14 m) long
Oceans

Euoplocephalus
(pp. 22–23)
ankylosaur
20 feet (6.1 m) long
North America

Gorgosaurus
(pp. 18–19)
tyrannosaur
30 feet (9.1 m) long
North America

Hesperornis
(pp. 16–17)
bird
6 feet (1.8 m) long
Oceans

Hypsilophodon
(pp. 6–7)
hypsilophodont
6.6 feet (2 m) long
Europe

Lambeosaurus
(pp. 18–19)
hadrosaur
31 feet (9.4 m) long
North America

Lurdusaurus
(pp. 10–11)
iguanodont
30 feet (9.1 m) long
Africa

Maiasaura
(pp. 20–21)
hadrosaur
30 feet (9.1 m) long
North America

Microraptor
(pp. 8–9)
dromaeosaur
3 feet (0.9 m) long
Asia

Mononykus
(pp. 24–25)
maniraptora
3.3 feet (1 m) long
Asia

Ouranosaurus
(pp. 10–11)
iguanodont
27 feet (8.2 m) long
Africa

Pachycephalosaurus
(pp. 28–29)
pachycephalosaur
15 feet (4.6 m) long
North America

Pachyrhinosaurus
(pp. 22–23)
ceratopsid
26 feet (7.9 m) long
North America

Pelecanimimus
(pp. 6–7)
ornithomimosaur
8 feet (2.4 m) long
Europe

Polacanthus
(pp. 6–7)
nodosaurid
16 feet (4.9 m) long
Europe

Protoceratops
(pp. 26–27)
ceratopsid
6.6 feet (2 m) long
Asia

Psittacosaurus
(pp. 8–9)
ceratopsid
6.6 feet (2 m) long
Asia

Quetzalcoatlus
(pp. 28–29)
pterosaur
36 feet (11 m)
North America

Saltasaurus
(pp. 4–5)
titanosaur
39 feet (11.9 m) long
South America

Sarcosuchus
(pp. 10–11)
crocodylomorph
39 feet (11.9 m) long
Africa, South America

Saurolophus
(pp. 22–23)
hadrosaur
32 feet (9.8 m) long
North America, Asia

Sauropelta
(pp. 12–13)
nodosaurid
16 feet (4.9 m) long
North America

Sauroposeidon
(pp. 12–13)
titanosaur
112 feet (34.1 m) long
North America

Skorpiovenator
(pp. 14–15)
abelisaur
30 feet (9.1 m) long
South America

Styracosaurus
(pp. 18–19)
ceratopsid
18 feet (5.5 m) long
North America

Tarbosaurus
(pp. 24–25)
tyrannosaur
40 feet (12.2 m) long
Asia

Tenontosaurus
(pp. 12–13)
iguanodont
26 feet (7.9 m) long
North America

Triceratops
(pp. 28–29)
ceratopsid
29 feet (8.8 m) long
North America

Tylosaurus
(pp. 16–17)
mosasaur
49 feet (14.9 m) long
Oceans

Zhenyuanopterus
(pp. 8–9)
pterosaur
13.1 feet (4 m)
Asia

Glossary

abelisaur Large carnivorous theropods with useless arms.

ammonite Spiral-shaped sea creature belonging to the mollusk family.

ankylosaur Herbivorous dinosaurs with armor made of thick skin and bony nodules.

carnivore Meat-eating animal.

carnosaur Member of the allosaurs and their closest family.

carrion The dead flesh of an animal.

ceratopsid Herbivorous dinosaurs with elaborate horns and frills.

Cretaceous–Paleogene (K-Pg) extinction event One of the major extinction events that occurred 65 million years ago caused by a massive asteroid or comet hitting Earth.

crocodylomorphs An important group of reptiles that includes the crocodiles.

dromaeosaur Small to medium-sized feathered carnivorous dinosaurs with a sickle-shaped killing claw.

fossils The remains of living things that have turned to rock.

hadrosaurs Herbivorous dinosaurs also known as the duck-billed dinosaurs.

herbivore Plant-eating animal.

ichthyosaur A giant marine reptile that resembled a dolphin.

iguanodont Herbivorous dinosaur that walked on two legs. They typically had beak-like mouths and a spiked thumb.

maniraptora The group of animals that evolved into birds. It includes dinosaurs.

mosasaur Large, extinct, marine reptile.

nodosaurid Armored, herbivorous dinosaurs belonging to the ankylosaurids.

omnivore An animal that eats both meat and plants.

ornithischian A type of dinosaur that had a pelvis that was bird-hipped.

ornithomimosaur Dinosaurs which looked like modern ostriches.

ornithopod A type of dinosaur that became one of the most successful groups of herbivores in the Cretaceous.

oviraptorid Omnivorous theropod with a toothless, parrot-like beak.

pachycephalosaur Herbivorous dinosaurs with thick, domed skulls.

paleontologist A person who studies forms of life existing in prehistoric times by examining fossils.

plesiosaur A marine reptile that had four flippers, a short tail and a long neck.

pterosaur A flying reptile.

sauropod Herbivorous dinosaur with a long neck and tail that walked on all fours.

spinosaurid Large predators with crocodile-like skulls and conical teeth.

therizinosaur Bipedal dinosaurs with large claws on their hands.

theropods Dinosaurs that moved on two legs. Most of them were carnivorous.

titanosaur Sauropod dinosaurs that included some of the heaviest creatures ever to walk the Earth.

tyrannosaur Carnivorous dinosaurs of which T. rex is the best known.

Index